Waiting in Joyful Hope

Daily Reflections for
Advent and Christmas
2010–2011

Bishop Robert F. Morneau

LITURGICAL PRESS

Collegeville, Minnesota

www.litpress.org

Nihil Obstat: Rev. Robert C. Harren, *Censor deputatus.*

Imprimatur: ✚ Most Reverend John F. Kinney, J.C.D., D.D., Bishop of St. Cloud, Minnesota, November 6, 2009.

Cover design by Ann Blattner. Photo courtesy of PhotoSpin.com.

In addition to the optional memorial of St. Thomas Becket, there are other optional memorials not noted.

ISSN 1550-803X

ISBN: 978-0-8146-3083-9

Introduction

In the book of Hebrews we read, ". . . persevere in running the race that lies before us while keeping our eyes fixed on Jesus, the leader and perfecter of faith" (12:1b-2a). What great Advent advice! We are to fix our eyes on Jesus, the one who inspires and perfects the great gift of faith. It is Jesus who is coming again in new ways to call us to be disciples and stewards of God's many gifts.

Yet, we struggle to keep focused. So many distractions bombard our lives to such an extent that we become disoriented, yes, even lost in the cosmos. Even though Jesus comes in Scripture and sacraments, in community and in the poor, in the stirrings of our hearts, we often fail to register and respond to these many "advents."

We need not despair nor be discouraged. Each day is a new beginning; each liturgical season is another invitation to encounter God's grace made present and manifest in the miracle of the incarnation. Humbly we invoke the guidance of the Holy Spirit, a Spirit that enlightens us to see, a Spirit that enkindles us to love, and a Spirit that empowers us to hear and follow the voice of the Good Shepherd. We are not alone on this perilous journey. We travel together as a faith community and we have been promised the gift of the Lord's presence.

A prayerful pondering of the daily readings of Advent is one way of keeping our eyes fixed on Jesus. Sacred Scripture,

God's glorious revelation, is a gateway into the mind and heart of our Creator, Redeemer, and Sanctifier. Through gentle contemplation we "see" God's providential love and mercy revealed in the person of Jesus. It is his coming for which we prepare with wonder and awe. Hospitality is the grace needed; a warm and gracious welcome is our gift to the newborn King.

Mary kept her eyes fixed on Jesus. It was her faith, obedience, and love that so influenced salvation history. Mary's *fiat*, her graced yes to the angel Gabriel, models for us Advent people the disposition necessary for our participation in the paschal mystery. So many have emulated Mary in her obedience: the great St. Paul, St. Thérèse of Lisieux, Blessed Teresa of Calcutta, St. Ignatius of Loyola. They all fixed their eyes on Jesus and followed in his way of love, compassion, and forgiveness.

As we attempt to keep our eyes fixed on Jesus, let us never forget that God's gaze is always upon us. As St. John of the Cross reminds us, when God looks, God loves and gives life. During Advent we are first seen and, because of that, we are enabled to fix our eyes on the great miracle of the incarnation.

FIRST WEEK OF ADVENT

Eat, Drink, and Be Merry

Readings: Isa 2:1-5; Rom 13:11-14; Matt 24:37-44

Scripture:
"In those days before the flood,
  they were eating and drinking,
  marrying and giving in marriage,
  up to the day that Noah entered the ark." (Matt 24:38)

Reflection: In the eighth chapter of the book of Ecclesiastes, the author sees vanity and emptiness all over the place. Almost to the point of disgust, the author exasperatingly proclaims that under our sun, on this planet Earth, there is nothing good except eating, drinking, and mirth (Eccl 8:15). Apparently the people in Noah's days followed this philosophy and were eating, drinking, and "marrying" right up to the time of the flood. They did not take seriously the "seriousness" of this life.

St. Paul attacks the narrow philosophy that sees good only in eating-drinking-being merry. His categories to describe such a lifestyle are orgies and drunkenness, promiscuity and lust, rivalry and jealousy. By spending most of our time making "provision[s] for the desires of the flesh," our very salvation is endangered. Paul's philosophy (indeed, his theology) is that we build our lives in God through the person of Jesus. When Christ is the cornerstone, our eating, drinking, and mirth will be ordered and will lead to peace rather than to chaos.

On the mountain of the Lord, claims Isaiah the prophet, we are given a philosophy of peace and unity. The beautiful metaphors of spears being transformed into pruning hooks and swords into plowshares offer us a way of life that is not centered on violence and the desires of the flesh. By walking in the path of the Lord we ascend God's mountain and experience God's intimacy and friendship.

"Eat, drink, and be merry!" These human activities are foundational and must be respected. But if they are the central values of one's life, trouble is around the corner: obesity, drunkenness, dissipation. If they are experienced in moderation and subordinate to God's way, they are a graced source of appropriate delight and pleasure.

Meditation: How do you handle the desires of the flesh and the desires of the spirit? How does fasting help us to prepare for the Lord's coming?

Prayer: Lord Jesus, as we begin our Advent journey, grant us your wisdom. May we see what is truly important and deeply live your values. Keep us mindful of your presence. May we be grateful for your gift of love and salvation. Come, Lord Jesus, come.

Advent Compassion and Humility

Readings: Isa 4:2-6; Matt 8:5-11

Scripture:
The centurion said in reply,
"Lord, I am not worthy to have you enter under my roof;
only say the word and my servant will be healed."
    (Matt 8:8)

Reflection: When we receive the Eucharist, when Jesus enters under our roof, is our primary motive spiritual comfort and consolation or is our focus on a deeper participation in the life of the Lord? Mature Christians receive Communion so that they might enter more fully into the life-giving ministry of Jesus.

The centurion was deeply concerned about his servant who was suffering dreadfully. Obviously, the centurion was a man of compassion as he strove to assist his servant by imploring the Lord's help. But the centurion was also a man of humility. In the presence of the Christ, the official knew himself unworthy of such a divine guest. And third, the centurion was a man of faith, a faith that impressed Jesus to such an extent that he refers to sitting at a banquet with such believers as Abraham, Isaac, and Jacob. It doesn't get any better than that.

Back home, the servant is paralyzed and suffering. Probably the whole purpose of Jesus' coming to Capernaum was to encounter the centurion who in turn would invite Jesus to come to his house so that the servant might be cured. Anyone who has suffered dreadful pain or experienced paralysis can appreciate what it means to hear the approaching feet of a healing physician. Tears of joy and gratitude must have flooded the servant's heart and soul.

The prophet Isaiah speaks of the glory of the Lord, God's love made radiant and visible. That glory is made manifest, according to Isaiah, when the Lord washes away our sins and purges us of our guilt and shame. Where there was darkness, now there is light, a flaming fire; where there was lostness and fear, a cloud guides the people in the way of the Lord. God is faithful to his creative, redeeming, sanctifying love.

Meditation: What is your central motive in receiving the Lord in the Eucharist? How does the reception of Communion affect the rest of your day?

Prayer: Lord Jesus, give us the grace of compassion and humility. May we feel deeply the pain of others; may we be aware of our unworthiness. Deepen our Advent faith so that our waiting may be both patient and filled with joy.

Tuesday of the First Week of Advent
(Episcopal Church)

Red-Hot Iron

Readings: Rom 10:9-18; Matt 4:18-22

Scripture:
He [Jesus] said to them,
   "Come after me, and I will make you fishers of men."
At once they left their nets and followed him. (Matt 4:19-20)

Reflection: Adverbs play a significant role in life, adverbs such as "at once" and "immediately." These words describe the manner in which Peter and Andrew, James and John, responded to the Lord's call of discipleship. "At once they left their nets" and "immediately they left their boat" and followed Jesus. We have here an example of the urgency of the Gospel call.

There is an expression: "Strike when the iron is hot." Blacksmiths have a hard time working with cold iron but once that iron is plunged into the forge and heated, crafting begins. Jesus saw in Peter and Andrew, in James and John, some red-hot iron. He struck them with that "Come after me" hammer and their lives changed forever. We are now the beneficiaries of their loving response.

St. Paul responded to the call of discipleship in a more delayed fashion than Peter and Andrew, than the sons of Zebedee. But respond he did and in a complete and sacrificial way. Like St. Andrew, the apostle Paul was sent to proclaim the mysteries of faith. Paul reminds us that faith comes from hearing, and who will hear if no one is sent? Once Paul encountered Christ, his soul was red-hot and burning with zeal. Once Paul saw the light, he ignited the hearts of the Gentile nation.

In our opening prayer for today's feast we pray: "You called Andrew the apostle / to preach the gospel and guide your Church in faith. / May he always be our friend in your presence / to help us with his prayers."

May we also ask St. Andrew to aid us to respond immediately (at once) whenever the Lord calls us. May we not hesitate out of fear or procrastinate out of laziness. Rather, may the Holy Spirit make us red-hot instruments of God's message of love and mercy.

Meditation: What are three or four major adverbs in your life? Immediately? Lovingly? Compassionately? Sullenly? Hopefully? In what sense do adverbs color our days?

Prayer: St. Andrew, may we witness to the Gospel by our lives. Jesus calls us to follow in his way today. May our response be immediate and total; may our discipleship be unreserved and joyful. May no attachment, be it to a person or things, prevent us from doing God's will.

The Hungers of the Human Spirit

Readings: Isa 25:6-10a; Matt 15:29-37

Scripture:
Jesus summoned his disciples and said,
  "My heart is moved with pity for the crowd,
  for they have been with me now for three days
  and have nothing to eat." (Matt 15:32a)

Reflection: As a pilgrim people we have many hungers. Basic to survival are food and drink. Basic to our psychological and spiritual health are love and grace. Unless these hungers are satisfied we become ill and face death. Add to this our hunger for spiritual fulfillment, union with our loving God.

Our two readings for today are filled with food and drink. Isaiah speaks of "juicy, rich food and pure, choice wines." Jesus takes the seven loaves and the fish and feeds a multitude of people.

But then Isaiah speaks about tears being wiped away and the divine reproach being removed from the people. Jesus cures the lame, the blind, the deformed, and the mute, giving people new life and purpose.

All of this flows out of divine pity, our God who loves us and has compassion on our weaknesses and needs. Our Advent call is to go to the mountain and to encounter the living and true God revealed in Jesus. We can be assured that Jesus will not send us away hungry but will fulfill our deepest longings. The same God revealed in Jesus inspired Isaiah to offer a vision of God's compassion. Put very simply, God will provide for all that we need. Divine providence leads us to rejoice in our salvation.

Through our participation in the sacramental life of the church, each one of us becomes involved in God's divine pity and compassion. We are to share our bread and fish, our rich food and choice wines, with others. We are to support our medical personnel as they assist the blind and lame, restoring them to health. We must not allow people to go away hungry when our tables are full and our money is making interest in the market.

By putting on the mind and heart of Christ this Advent we can make sure that, come Christmas Eve, there will be at least seven baskets of fragments left over.

Meditation: How do you participate in the saving mission of Jesus? What are the hungers of your heart?

Prayer: Lord Jesus, stir up in our hearts the flame of compassion. May we be sensitive to the needs of others and responsive to situations. We have been so blessed. May we share your gifts with others and fulfill their every hunger.

Obedience: The Path to Peace

Readings: Isa 26:1-6; Matt 7:21, 24-27

Scripture:
Jesus said to his disciples:
"Not everyone who says to me, 'Lord, Lord,'
   will enter the Kingdom of heaven,
   but only the one who does the will of my Father in
      heaven." (Matt 7:21)

Reflection: One of the central paradoxes of spirituality is that our true liberty is found in obedience. We become "free" only when we do the will of God. More, we experience peace to the extent that we listen and respond to the movements of grace. This concept of freedom is far distant from our current philosophy, which says that freedom means doing whatever we want to do.

The gospel presents two types of individuals: the wise person and the fool. Indeed, how foolish it is to build one's house on sand. By contrast, intelligence is shown when our residence is constructed on solid rock. Isaiah the prophet speaks about the Lord being "an eternal Rock." To build our lives on our relationship with God is a very smart thing to do. When the trials and tribulations of life come, as they surely will, we will not be swept away. Our trust is in God and God's will, not in our own agenda and power.

Here is a ruling thought for our Advent season: "To obey the inspirations of grace moment by moment, adjusting oneself readily to the promptings of a living Master, is a task that demands the glorious liberty that is the high prerogative of the children of God." The grace needed here is docility to the gifts of the Holy Spirit.

In Western culture there are few values more highly treasured than freedom. That freedom is often described as the ability to do whatever we want to do. And infringement on our liberty is to be questioned. Yet, how "free" are we in this culture "possessed" by consumerism, materialism, and relativism? True freedom lies in obedience to what we *ought* to do and that *ought* is grounded in the will of God.

Meditation: What is your working definition of freedom? Are there any areas in your life—physical, emotional, moral, spiritual—where you are not free?

Prayer: God of freedom and peace, instill in us a love of your will. In it is our peace; in it is our joy. By living your words of love, compassion, and forgiveness, we come to be what we are called to be: people of the light. Do not allow us to use our liberty to walk in darkness and sin. Come, Lord Jesus, come.

December 3: Feast of Saint Francis Xavier
(Catholic Church)

Friday of the First Week of Advent
(Episcopal Church)

The Cry of Faith

Readings: Isa 29:17-24; Matt 9:27-31

Scripture:
As Jesus passed by, two blind men followed him, crying
out,
"Son of David, have pity on us!" (Matt 9:27)

Reflection: The Lord asked the blind men if they believed in his power to cure them. After giving their affirmative response, they were healed and ventured forth proclaiming this deed even though Jesus warned them not to do so. It's as if the healed men invoked the hymn "How Can [We] Keep from Singing."

Jesus responded to the cry of faith. Our world today struggles with so much blindness and deafness. We fail to see reality for what it is; we fail to hear the cry of the poor and brokenhearted. Until we cry out, "Son of David, have pity on us!" and do so with deep faith, nothing will change. We do not have it within ourselves to bring about healing; nor do the promises of science and psychology have the capacity to bring about the transformation needed to make us a new creation.

Isaiah had faith. He tells us the deaf will hear, the blind will see, the lowly will find joy, the poor will have their fill. One day the tyrant will be no more and evil will be conquered. Because of the power of God we will be given understanding and the gift of reverence. Isaiah knew well the realities of his day. There were tyrannies and evil; there were many poor and lowly who were oppressed and depressed. Yet, the prophet believed in God's goodness and power and offered an alternative reality to what "is." Isaiah's faith has inspired us for thousands of years.

Back in the nineteenth century, the American essayist Ralph Waldo Emerson wrote, "The disease with which the human mind now labors is want of faith." Emerson's observation is not limited to his own day. Every age struggles with a want of faith, and until we realize our blindness, that want will never be satisfied.

Meditation: Is our age one characterized by a "want of faith"? What is your understanding of the theological virtue of faith? Talk to someone you know who is a faith-filled person.

Prayer: Lord Jesus, Son of David and Son of Mary, have pity on all of us who suffer from spiritual blindness and deafness. We truly believe that you have the power to heal and restore us to the fullness of life. We truly believe in your love and pity. Come, Lord Jesus, come.

Gift, Gratitude, Generosity: The Three Big Gs

Readings: Isa 30:19-21, 23-26; Matt 9:35–10:1, 5a, 6-8

Scripture:
"Without cost you have received; without cost you are to
    give." (Matt 10:8b)

Reflection: Near our family home there was an electrical
transforming station. From towering power lines energy
would come streaming into the station, to be "transformed"
into lesser voltage, and sent on its merry way to businesses
and homes. I always stood in admiration of this technology
of receiving and transmitting, retaining nothing for itself. It
became a metaphor for me of the Christian life: we are to be
recipients and transmitters of God's energy, which we call
grace.

Jesus gave the grace of healing and teaching to the disciples. This gift was given for the sake of others, those who
were ill, possessed, or ignorant. With gratitude in their
hearts, the disciples generously shared the blessings given
to them. They exercised stewardship, the receiving, nurturing, and sharing of God's gifts.

But there seems to be a problem in all of this divine generosity since Jesus is aware of so many people who lack a
shepherd. Has God's grace dried up? Are the gifts of healing
and teaching no longer available to our times? Why is there

a shortage of laborers when we know full well that God's call and lavish generosity are still operative?

For various reasons, the hearts of people are no longer moved with pity when they see the needy. For diverse reasons, gifts offered by God are not received and shared. Even though the reign of God is at hand, there is a lack of response to God's continual initiative. Is the reason for refusing the vocation of being recipients and transmitters of God's grace sheer stubbornness, or want of interest in God's concerns, or blatant narcissism? Whatever the cause, the flow of grace is checked when we refuse to respond to God's will.

Isaiah was a gifted prophet; Isaiah was grateful for graces received; Isaiah generously did the work of the Lord in proclaiming God as gracious and loving. Here is one transformer and laborer in the harvest who received and shared God's very life.

Meditation: Can you identify with being a recipient and transmitter of God's grace? What is your level of gratitude and generosity? Send a note of gratitude to someone you consider to be a laborer in the harvest.

Prayer: Generous God, all is gift. You invite us every moment of every day to participate in your life of self-giving. Help us to be agents of your light, your love, and your life. Do not let us check the flow of grace by sin and selfishness. May we do the work you have assigned us in your great harvest.

SECOND WEEK OF ADVENT

Justice and Faithfulness

Readings: Isa 11:1-10; Rom 15:4-9; Matt 3:1-12

Scripture:
Justice shall be the band around his waist,
    and faithfulness a belt upon his hips. (Isa 11:5)

Reflection: If one were to write a biography of John the Baptist, a number of attributes would stand out. Courage would be close to the top of the list as John fearlessly took on Herod and his immoral lifestyle. Another attribute of the Baptist would be discipline, for here was one who ate locusts and wild honey and dressed in camel's hair. Surely, honesty would have to be mentioned, as John confronts the Pharisees and Sadducees with the harsh reality that they were comparable to a brood of vipers. Throw into this mix John's poetic bent, as he uses analogies and metaphors to teach the lessons of life.

If Isaiah the prophet were John's biographer, would he not proclaim this about the Baptist: "Justice shall be the band round his waist, / and faithfulness a belt upon his hips" (Isa 11:5)? The Baptist was a just man, living out the obligations given him and honoring the rights of others. His duty was that of preparing the way for that Someone mightier than himself and deserving of total allegiance. John the Baptist honored others, including the Pharisees and Sadducees, by giving them the truth of who they were and what they were doing.

The Baptist was also faithful. Whether or not people listened and responded to his message of repentance, the preaching would be done. We, twenty-one centuries later, still hear that voice from the desert announcing the Lord's coming and the need to make straight God's royal road. John's single-mindedness, a subcategory of faithfulness, focused on the kingdom of heaven.

In our contemporary culture, two major forces oppose the call to Advent justice and Advent faithfulness. Those forces are relativism and pluralism. John the Baptist, as well as St. Paul, maintained a standard of what is good and just, and they did not deviate from that criterion. Whatever is pleasing to God and whatever fosters the kingdom is good; whatever displeases God or blocks the kingdom from coming is evil. Their ethics of justice and righteousness were firm. No relativism here.

And both Paul and John refused the pluralism that claims that there is no truth. Both of these disciples found God's truthfulness in the person of Jesus. In him was the justice and faithfulness of God.

Meditation: What would your biographer list as your major attributes? Would justice and faithfulness be on the list? Spend some Advent time reflecting on your gifts and weaknesses.

Prayer: John the Baptist, pray that we, as a church, may be just in all our transactions and faithful in doing God's will. May we also be given the courage to be true disciples of the Lord Jesus. May hope sustain us in our trials and tribulations. Thank you for preparing the way of the Lord.

Thoughts of the Heart

Readings: Isa 35:1-10; Luke 5:17-26

Scripture:
Jesus knew their thoughts and said to them in reply,
 "What are you thinking in your hearts?" (Luke 5:22)

Reflection: Privacy is a value of supreme importance. Most of us are very protective of our personal lives and resist any trespassing whatsoever. When others learn our thoughts and feelings without our consent, we become nervous, if not resentful. That is why we can be very uncomfortable when someone can read our minds and discern our feelings.

The scribes and Pharisees in today's gospel saw Jesus' healing ministry as blasphemy since only God can forgive sins and save people from spiritual death. What a surprise to them that Jesus could read their thoughts. What a challenge when Jesus questioned them for thinking such thoughts in their hearts. Of course, Jesus also was aware that the thoughts of the scribes and Pharisees were not limited to the questioning of forgiveness of sins, they were questioning whether Jesus should be allowed to live. Yet one wonders how those Pharisees and scribes could not have been seized with astonishment when the paralyzed man picked up his stretcher and headed home.

By contrast, we are given entrance into what Isaiah was thinking in his heart. Once again it is about God's glory and how the weak will be made strong and the frightened will be given courage. Isaiah was even thinking about how the desert will be watered and how people will be ransomed and redeemed. Here are thoughts of peace, love, and joy.

The gospel question—"What are you thinking in your hearts?"—should haunt us day and night. Thoughts matter, especially thoughts of the heart. We need the Spirit of Jesus to purify our minds and hearts and to fill them with gentle, wise, and loving thoughts and feelings.

In Henrik Ibsen's play *Hedda Gabler*, Hedda comments: "One is not always mistress of one's thoughts." Thoughts and feelings often come uninvited. Our Advent task is to monitor them and discern what is and what is not of the Lord, and then respond appropriately.

Meditation: What are the thoughts of your heart? Spend some time journaling at night and jotting down the feelings and thoughts of the day. How much do thoughts matter?

Prayer: Lord Jesus, you know our mind and our heart. Nothing is hidden from your gaze. Send your Spirit to purify our inner lives. Give us gentle spirits that we might express your love and think your thoughts. Come, Lord Jesus, come.

December 7: Saint Ambrose
(Catholic Church)

Tuesday of the Second Week of Advent
(Episcopal Church)

The Stray

Readings: Isa 40:1-11; Matt 18:12-14

Scripture:
"What is your opinion?
If a man has a hundred sheep and one of them goes astray,
    will he not leave the ninety-nine in the hills
    and go in search of the stray?" (Matt 18:12)

Reflection: In his autobiographical reflections *All the Strange Hours*, Loren Eiseley, a paleontologist and a powerful prose writer, questions why humans beat and starve small things. He tells of looking into the eyes of a starved mongrel and being unable to forget that animal's plight. Here is a man of compassion, sensitive to creatures who experience that painful reality of being a stray and lost.

Jesus calls our attention to a single sheep that has strayed from the flock. He poses the question of how much value this single creature has in the eyes and heart of the shepherd. We know the Lord's response. More, we know that it is a story about us who, in sin, stray from God and distance ourselves from one another. And then the amazing lavishness of God's love: Jesus will leave all in pursuit of us. Here is the Good Shepherd who recognizes the value and dignity of every sheep.

Isaiah also refers to the shepherd/sheep theme. The prophet informs us that God is like a shepherd who feeds the flock, gathers the lambs into his arms, and carries them close to his heart. All this is done with care and compassion. Jesus takes the image of the shepherd a step further in presenting the case of the sheep that has strayed. It is God's will that none be lost. Such is God's commitment that he sends his only Son to seek us out and find us. As disciples of this Beloved Son, we are to do the same: seek out and bring home those who have wandered far from the faith.

If anyone were to argue that the shepherd would be unwise to leave the ninety-nine in the hills and go in search of a single sheep, we might be reminded that in reality all of us have strayed to one degree or another. In fact, there are no ninety-nine to leave in the hills because they have all drifted to some degree from God's loving embrace. All this translates to the fact that we all need redemption.

Meditation: What is your reaction when you see a stray dog or cat? What is your reaction to the people who are on the margins of society and are lost?

Prayer: Jesus, our Good Shepherd, gather us once again into your loving embrace. Feed us with the gift of life, the Eucharist, and fill our hearts with compassion for all who are lost. May we reach out to those who have strayed and bring them back into your presence. Help us to build your kingdom of justice and peace.

Chosen and Consecrated

Readings: Gen 3:9-15, 20; Eph 1:3-6, 11-12; Luke 1:26-38

Scripture:
In him we were also chosen,
   destined in accord with the purpose of the One
   who accomplishes all things according to the intention
    of his will. (Eph 1:11)

Reflection: There are two faith events in our tradition that are supreme examples of surrender to God's will: Jesus in the garden at Gethsemane and Mary's great yes to the message from the angel Gabriel. Because Mary and Jesus knew themselves chosen by the Father, they in turn consecrated themselves to do God's will, whatever the price. And we know what that price was: total self-emptying. Jesus died on the cross; Mary's heart was pierced by a sword.

In 1967, Chaim Potok's novel *The Chosen* was a bestseller. It is a story of the friendship of two Jewish youths, even though they are raised in very different Jewish traditions. Despite the difference in training and formation, the two youths, Reuven Malter and Danny Saunders, choose to be friends. By so doing it changes their lives. Friendship sometimes simply happens, at other times it comes by way of intentional choice.

Friendship with God is another name for grace or charity. God chose Mary even before she gave birth to the Anointed One. "No stain of Adam's sin" touched her and Mary accepted her chosenness and eventually consecrated her life to the mystery of salvation. The consecration was a total self-offering to God's concerns and purpose. God chose Mary; Mary chose to do God's will.

In baptism, all of us have been chosen as well. The question remains as to the degree of consecration we will make. Because of freedom, we can give or withhold ourselves from this commitment of the gift of self. Mary and Jesus surrendered their wills to what the Father asked. We are invited and empowered by the Holy Spirit to do the same. This self-transcendent love is only possible through divine grace.

Meditation: What is your understanding of consecration? In what sense have you been chosen? Reflect on the people you have met who have consecrated their lives to God's purposes.

Prayer: Mary, the chosen one, pray that our minds and hearts may be open to the wisdom and love of God. Intercede for us that we may dedicate our lives to furthering the kingdom of God. We know that we have been chosen in grace; we hope that we might have the grace to say yes to whatever the Lord asks.

December 9: Saint Juan Diego
(Catholic Church, optional memorial)

Thursday of the Second Week of Advent
(Episcopal Church)

Taken by the Hand

Readings: Isa 41:13-20; Matt 11:11-15

Scripture:
I am the LORD, your God,
   who grasp your right hand;
It is I who say to you, "Fear not,
   I will help you." (Isa 41:13)

Reflection: George Herbert (1593–1633), the Anglican priest-poet, titles one of his poems "Love (III)." Here is Herbert's concept of God: a God who invites us into divine life, a God who will not be put off with our excuse of not being worthy or grateful, a God who demands that we sit at the divine table and taste of the divine food. There is one line in the poem that Isaiah the prophet would especially appreciate: "Love took my hand, and smiling did reply, / Who made the eyes but I?" We are grasped by a loving, redeeming God.

   God took Juan Diego by the hand when, in December of 1531 while on his way to Mass, Juan encountered Mary, the Mother of God. From this experience, the church was given the great devotion to Our Lady of Guadalupe. God's invitation comes out of the blue. Our challenge is to be open to the Lord's voice and to be willing to be taken by the hand. Much faith and trust is demanded here.

John the Baptist, whom Jesus identifies as none greater born of women, was taken by the hand. This "violent" one, along with other prophets like Elijah and Isaiah, used strong language to stir the people to repentance. We hear Isaiah's "violent" language of "worm" and "maggot" that challenges people to turn to a God who is gracious, merciful, slow to anger, and rich in kindness.

The God who takes us by the hand this Advent is a God who smiles in love at his poor, weak creatures. This Advent God takes delight in us, his people. This is a truly amazing grace, the gratuitous love of an extravagant God revealed in Jesus. May we never take this gift of friendship for granted.

Meditation: How has the Lord taken you by the hand? Do you consider the prophets violent? Is this necessarily a negative thing? When has the Lord invited you to sit at the divine table?

Prayer: Lord Jesus, help us to understand that the kingdom of heaven suffers violence. Give us the grace to be taken by the hand and led where you want us to go. Too often we go it alone and get lost time and time again. Come, Lord Jesus, come.

Coaching

Readings: Isa 48:17-19; Matt 11:16-19

Scripture:
Thus says the LORD, your redeemer,
    the Holy One of Israel:
I, the LORD, your God,
    teach you what is for your good,
    and lead you on the way you should go. (Isa 48:17)

Reflection: In almost every area of business and education, the concept of coaching has become popular. Inexperienced employees are given assistance by professional staff to develop their talent and correct bad practices. Many individuals have grown personally through this tutoring and hands-on mentoring.

But this coaching has always been a part of our Judeo-Christian tradition. Isaiah the prophet speaks about a redeeming God who instructs us in the ways of goodness and prosperity. Our task is to understand and live the commandments. The question always remains: are we coachable? Another question: do we really want to change and do we believe that change is possible? Until we respond positively to these questions, no amount of coaching will be to much avail.

In Jesus' generation there seems to have been a problem just like in our own times. Flutes were played but people did not dance; dirges were sung but no one mourned. They just didn't get it. And one can sense the frustration in Jesus' voice as he uses the example of eating and drinking. John did not eat or drink and was accused of being possessed; Jesus did eat and drink and was labeled a glutton and a drunkard. How many tutors, mentors, and coaches were needed to help the people see reality for what it is?

And our generation? We are just as dense. There is no lack of instructors or teachers in our day, but perhaps there is a lack of witnesses. We will be open to coaching to the extent that our mentors and tutors live what they teach. God calls us to be instruments of his wisdom. If we are to coach, we must also live the commandments. Pope Paul VI, in his great letter on evangelization, stressed time and time again the need for us to live the Gospel, that we may witness to the way of Jesus—the way of love, compassion, and forgiveness.

Meditation: Who are the people who coached you in the ways of the Lord? Did they also live the message they conveyed? Whom has God asked you to coach?

Prayer: Lord Jesus, open our minds and hearts to your message and to your messengers. We stand in need of knowledge and understanding, in need of authentic living of your word. Guide us in your ways always.

Elijah and John the Baptist

Readings: Sir 48:1-4, 9-11; Matt 17:9a, 10-13

Scripture:
In those days,
like a fire there appeared the prophet Elijah
   whose words were as a flaming furnace. (Sir 48:1)

Reflection: In divine graciousness, God keeps sending us messengers to remind us of what is important in life. We, too often, are so fussy, worrying about unnecessary details and getting caught up in the nonessential. The prophets cut through to the heart of the matter and draw our attention to God's interests and concerns. Long before books on effective habits were written, the prophets knew to "put first things first." During Advent it might be profitable to read the prophets, rather than management books, to find out about effectiveness and efficiency.

Elijah and John the Baptist were effective and efficient. They came with flaming words that called all of us to conversion of mind and heart. These prophets were sensitive to sin, our turning away from God and one another. Prophets confront our narrowness of heart, our intolerance and narcissism, our prejudices and impatience, our enslavement to passion and undisciplined lives. It is not surprising that they were rejected, yes, executed in many cases. The truth they proclaimed was too much to bear.

Prophets refused to flatter human nature with a philosophy of "I'm okay, you're okay!" On the contrary, they were sent to point out that God's love is so great and purifying that God will not leave us in our unredeemed state. Generation after generation, heralds emerge to make us look honestly at our beauty and our ugliness. And finally, after all the Elijahs and John the Baptists, comes Jesus whose love and mercy cleanses us of our brokenness. All we have to do is to surrender ourselves to his loving gaze and abide by his commands.

In our gospel acclamation we cry out: "Prepare the way of the Lord, make straight his paths: / All flesh shall see the salvation of God." We give thanks to God for Elijah and John the Baptist and Isaiah for preparing our minds and hearts to embrace God's salvation, the Lord Jesus.

Meditation: Who are the prophets in your life calling you to conversion of mind and heart? What is your understanding of human nature? Do you flatter it or call it to task?

Prayer: Lord Jesus, you are *the* prophet, indeed, our priest and king. Open our minds to your purposes and our hearts to your interests. May we turn from sin and embrace your tender mercies. Come, Lord Jesus, come.

THIRD WEEK OF ADVENT

December 12: Third Sunday of Advent

Two Advent Questions

Readings: Isa 35:1-6a, 10; Jas 5:7-10; Matt 11:2-11

Scripture:
"Are you the one who is to come,
or should we look for another?" . . .
"What did you go out to the desert to see?"
(Matt 11:3, 7b)

Reflection: John the Baptist and Jesus asked questions. The imprisoned John was looking for confirmation that Jesus was truly the Anointed One of God. The answer to his question was to be found, not in a yes or no response, but in the very ministry of Jesus. New life and hope were happening all over the place: the blind saw, the lame walked, the sick were cured, the dead were given new life, the poor heard good news. Indeed, Jesus was the one whom God had sent.

And Jesus asked the crowds what they were looking for in the person of the prophet John. Using metaphors and images, Jesus dismissed swaying reeds and regal clothing. Rather, John was a prophet sent with a message of preparation. John's work was done. Now he could return to the God who sent him.

But there is perhaps a third Advent question worth asking: what are we looking for in this Advent season? Or, to ask the question in another way: in what or in whom do we find that everlasting joy that Isaiah spoke of so eloquently? For Jesus, his joy lay in doing the will of the Father; for John, fulfilling his mission as a prophet brought him that peace that is beyond all understanding. All of us are looking for that happiness that is often synonymous with joy and peace. By following the example of the prophets, the prophet John, who bridged the Old and the New Testaments, and the example of Jesus, who is *the* prophet, we have the possibility of sharing in the glory of God's kingdom. Advent is a special liturgical season in which we can take a long, serious look at our role in furthering the kingdom of God.

Meditation: Do you find John the Baptist's question concerning Jesus to be startling? What did Jesus mean when he said that the least in God's kingdom is greater than John the Baptist?

Prayer: Lord Jesus, fill us with the joy that comes from doing the Father's will. May we emulate John the Baptist by being messengers of your love and mercy. May we imitate your compassion for others by serving those who are in need. Come, Lord Jesus, come.

December 13: Saint Lucy
(Catholic Church)

Monday of the Third Week of Advent
(Episcopal Church)

Authority

Readings: Num 24:2-7, 15-17a; Matt 21:23-27

Scripture:
When Jesus had come into the temple area,
  the chief priests and the elders of the people approached
    him
  as he was teaching and said,
  "By what authority are you doing these things?"
    (Matt 21:23)

Reflection: If you are a candidate for open-heart surgery, you might want to ask the operating surgeon by what authority does he propose to cut you open. The doctor would turn to the wall and point at a diploma granted by a certified medical institution. Behind that diploma are years and years of study, experience, and acquired skills. These qualifications give the doctor appropriate authority and should bring some peace of mind.

Jesus taught with authority. Although the gospel does not tell us the source of that authority, we know what it is by our faith: Jesus taught with conviction, certitude, and authority because it was given by the Father. It was an exercise of divine authority by a divine person. The chief priests and elders failed to focus on the message and tried to entrap Jesus by using the question of authority to protect their own status. Jesus would have none of this and even refused to get involved in their game.

In the first reading we see how God uses Balaam and his oracle as way of affirming Jacob and Israel. Balaam's authority does not arise from educational experience or from naïve intelligence. Rather, it is God's grace being mediated through the utterances of Balaam that instill hope in a people so easily discouraged.

Authority has fallen upon hard times in our culture. We live in an atmosphere of suspicion and lack of trust. Part of this is the result of authority betraying its trust; part of it is the fear of losing what one thinks is freedom. Authentic authority, exercised well, is a liberating and redemptive grace. Jesus used his power to free others and thereby save them.

Meditation: What is your attitude toward authority? What type of authority do you exercise? When is authority redemptive; when is it nonredemptive?

Prayer: Lord Jesus, you taught with authority. Open our minds to the truth of your message; open our hearts to the warmth of your love. May we come to realize that we are free to the extent that we live under your gracious authority. Continue to author us into life and make us fitting instruments of your authority in the lives of others.

December 14: Saint John of the Cross
(Catholic Church)

Tuesday of the Third Week of Advent
(Episcopal Church)

A Way of Holiness

Readings: Zeph 3:1-2, 9-13; Matt 21:28-32

Scripture:
"When John came to you in the way of righteousness,
    you did not believe him;
    but tax collectors and prostitutes did." (Matt 21:32a)

Reflection: St. John of the Cross (1542–1591) is considered one of the greatest writers on holiness in the church. Over the past four hundred years, thousands upon thousands of people have turned to him for guidance on the spiritual journey. John's teachings are clear and demanding, gentle and strong.

In one sense, he was very much like John the Baptist. St. John of the Cross realized the need for repentance, a turning from the darkness of sin to the light of God's grace. Holiness is grounded in truth and a significant part of truth is our failure to love and forgive people. So both John the Baptist and John of the Cross stressed the need for transformation by God's grace. Essentially, this way of holiness was the doing of God's will and a refusal to live a life of self-interest and self-indulgence.

Holiness is more than an intellectual assent to what God teaches through Scripture and the teachers in the church. Holiness is actually doing faith, putting into action the decrees of God. But there must be a radical awareness that holiness is rooted in one's relationship with God, fostered by prayer. Only when disciplined prayer and the offering of one's life in service come together are we on the road to holiness.

Apparently the tax collectors and prostitutes who listened to John the Baptist went on to live the message of repentance. Their faith was more than rational consent; it was doing God's will. The people in the time of St. John of the Cross found John's spirituality very demanding. Many did not believe in him because following what he said would demand a major change in lifestyle. But those who listened and followed John's way of holiness came to know the peace and joy of discipleship.

Meditation: What is your understanding of holiness? Would you agree with the theologian John Macquarrie that holiness is basically "obedience in a particular situation"? Reflect on the people in your life whom you consider to be walking the way of holiness.

Prayer: Lord Jesus, during this Advent time, you continue to call us to holiness. Help us to be listeners and lovers; help us to be obedient and self-giving. May the prayers of St. John the Baptist and St. John of the Cross help us to avoid discouragement. May their prayers help us to follow in your way of love, compassion, and forgiveness.

December 15: Wednesday of the Third Week of Advent

Expectations: Great and Small

Readings: Isa 45:6c-8, 18, 21c-25; Luke 7:18b-23

Scripture:
At that time,
John summoned two of his disciples and sent them to the
Lord to ask,
"Are you the one who is to come, or should we look
for another?" (Luke 7:18b-19)

Reflection: Clarifying expectations is an important task on
our faith journey. What does God expect of us? What do we
expect of God? Are our expectations realistic or neurotic?
Are they reasonable or romantic? Answers to these questions
shape our attitudes and our behavior.

John the Baptist asked if Jesus was the anointed of the Lord
or should the Baptist look elsewhere. Jesus does not give a
direct answer to the question. Rather, he tells John's disciples
to return and narrate what is happening to the blind and the
crippled, the sick and the deaf. New life is given to them;
hope is restored to their hearts. Jesus saves.

Elsewhere Jesus raises the question of expectations regarding John the Baptist. Did people go out to see him because
he was dressed in fine apparel or feasting on delicious food?
Jesus knew what John was about and tells the crowds that
John is indeed a prophet and more than a prophet. Our Lord
praises John for his greatness.

Advent is a season of expectation. We are a people awaiting the Lord's return, not only on the feast of the Lord's Nativity but also his coming into our daily lives. Our task is to recognize the intrusions of grace and to respond in an appropriate fashion. God does come in word and sacrament, in community and in the inner movements of our heart. We rightly expect these comings; God rightly expects that we open our minds and hearts to whatever is asked.

There is a rather sad line in Thomas Hardy's *The Return of the Native*: "As for Thomasin, I never expected much from her; and she has not disappointed me." Low expectations, small disappointment: high expectations, great disappointment. Perhaps not. We do expect great things from God and God will not disappoint us. And, God also expects great things of us. May we live up to his expectations for us.

Meditation: What are your expectations of God, yourself, and of life? Are these expectations realistic? Is it appropriate to have great expectations of God?

Prayer: Lord Jesus, you came to heal and set us free. John the Baptist heard of your work and came to know that you were the Messiah. Help us to be realistic in our expectations; help us to fulfill the expectations you have of us. Come, Lord Jesus, come.

God's Blessed Assurance

Readings: Isa 54:1-10; Luke 7:24-30

Scripture:
My love shall never leave you
  nor my covenant of peace be shaken,
    says the LORD, who has mercy on you. (Isa 54:10b)

Reflection: We need blessed assurance, an anchor that provides stability in a turbulent and changing world. Is there anyone or anything that we can count on, especially when trials and tribulations fall upon us? Isaiah the prophet provides an answer: God's love will never leave us nor can the great covenant of peace be shaken. This blessed assurance of love and peace flows out of God's immense mercy.

John the Baptist, imprisoned and awaiting execution, was given the gift of divine love by being called to the office of prophet. His ministry bridged the Old and New Testaments. John also knew the gift of peace for he aligned his will with that of God. John prepared the way of the Messiah, and Jesus acknowledged John's fidelity to the crowds. Through the mercy extended to John's parents, Elizabeth and Zechariah, salvation history took a step forward. Isaiah's prophecy was being fulfilled.

Though God's love and peace is offered, it need not be accepted. Some of the Pharisees and lawyers went in a different direction, opposing God's plan. God does not force the covenant on anyone. When this divine friendship is offered, people must make a decision to accept or reject it. And even if it is rejected, God's love and mercy is still available and is given as soon as an individual or community turns back to the Lord.

Jesus is the fulfillment of what Isaiah the prophet was talking about. Jesus is our peace; Jesus is the manifestation of God's love and mercy. Our Advent task is to open our minds and hearts to Christ's coming into our lives today. Once we have said yes to the divine invitation, then we are challenged to transmit the divine love, mercy, and peace to others. It's all about building the kingdom.

Isaiah speaks of God's love as enduring. This is a great consolation for us because we realize how shallow and often fickle our response can be. Our endurance is so limited; God's endurance and fidelity is infinite. This should give us consolation as we struggle to avoid sin and live a life of grace.

Meditation: Does your concept of God focus on the attributes of love and mercy? What do you understand by "blessed assurance?" In what ways can you regularly renew your covenant with the Lord?

Prayer: Lord Jesus, you admired John the Baptist and showered upon him your love and mercy. We too seek those graces; we too seek to live in the land of peace. Be with us in this Advent journey and heal our broken hearts.

December 17: Friday of the Third Week of Advent

Family of Origins

Readings: Gen 49:2, 8-10; Matt 1:1-17

Scripture:
The book of the genealogy of Jesus Christ,
    the son of David, the son of Abraham. (Matt 1:1)

Reflection: In the field of family counseling, professionals claim that to understand an individual, you must also have some understanding of their "family of origins." That is, who are the parents and grandparents? What about siblings and aunts and uncles? Are there any black sheep in the background? What are the ethnic and cultural factors that influenced that individual's formation? Until these questions are asked and answered, a counselor will not have a broad context in which to offer advice.

Matthew's gospel gives us the context of the life of Jesus, a genealogy that has noble and despicable characters. We hear of Solomon who was both wise and foolish; we hear of King David, a great leader and yet a murderer; we hear of Ahaz who would not tempt the Lord by asking for a sign. Also in Jesus' family tree are listed women who were part of his heritage: Ruth and Bathsheba and Mary, Jesus' own mother. All of these people made their unique contribution, for good or ill, to the story of salvation. We cannot understand who Jesus is without knowing something about his ancestors.

What is truly astonishing is that God uses the messiness of our historical condition to bring about our redemption. In his human nature, Jesus dealt with all the impulses and primitive instincts of his forefathers and foremothers. Our Lord took upon himself our temptations and struggles, our joys and hopes. The incarnation, the breaking of eternity into time, was a bloody affair. And, it was all done out of love.

As we draw near to the feast of our Lord's Nativity, we might reflect more deeply upon one ancestor of Jesus who models for us the gift of faith. That, of course, is father Abraham. He believed. He put his trust in God's word and what God promised him was fulfilled. His was a deep faith and required a mighty leap. Would that our faith were as strong and persevering.

Meditation: Do you find the genealogy of Jesus troublesome? Who is your favorite person in our Lord's family tree? Is your genealogy in any way similar to that of Jesus?

Prayer: Father Abraham, pray for us. Our faith is often shallow and tested by the winds of time. Intercede for us that we might be strong in embracing God's word, indeed, God's Word. Though we are often ignorant and have to contend with fear, help us to follow your example by doing whatever God asks of us.

December 18: Saturday of the Third Week of Advent

The Lord, Our Justice

Readings: Jer 23:5-8; Matt 1:18-25

Scripture:
In his days Judah shall be saved,
Israel shall dwell in security.
This is the name they give him:
"The LORD our justice." (Jer 23:6)

Reflection: When we think of justice, moral principles that demand action come to mind. One principle is the dignity of every single human being. Justice is done when that dignity is protected and promoted. Take the principle of preferential option for the poor in which those who are most needy have a special claim on our time and resources. Justice is about fulfilling one's obligations and respecting the rights of others.

But there is a deeper, more personal dimension to justice. Joseph was a just man, righteous and honest. Justice is so much more than the living out of ethical norms. It is a quality of the heart that embraces both compassion and truthfulness. Justice orders life according to God's design.

Thus, the prophet Jeremiah proclaims that the Lord himself is our justice. Here is a divine attribute that assures us that our rights will be reverenced. God is fair in dealing with us, knowing the degree of our responsibility as well as being aware of our overwhelming limitations. Because of this, God's justice can also be described as God's mercy. There is no strict and narrow imposition of punishment when our God is one of infinite love and forgiveness.

It was unto Mary that our Lord of justice and mercy was born. Jesus, the one who saves, and Emmanuel, God is with us, incarnates what might appear to be an abstract virtue. Now, through the incarnation and nativity of Christ, we see salvation, righteousness, justice, and mercy. These qualities have a face. And Mary and Joseph were instrumental in furthering God's providential design. Because of God's grace, justice will flourish in our time and the fullness of peace forever.

Meditation: What is your understanding of justice? Are God's justice and mercy distinct? When have you been an agent of justice? Who are the righteous people in your life who have incarnated God's peace?

Prayer: Lord Jesus, our justice and our peace, send forth your Spirit into our broken lives and world. We stand in need of your wisdom; we long to do the works of justice. Make us instruments of your peace. Come, Lord Jesus, come.

FOURTH WEEK OF ADVENT

Obedience of Faith

Readings: Isa 7:10-14; Rom 1:1-7; Matt 1:18-24

Scripture:
When Joseph awoke,
  he did as the angel of the Lord had commanded him
  and took his wife into his home. (Matt 1:24)

Reflection: Whether or not the gospel passage for today could be ranked as equal in importance to Mary's "May it be done to me according to your word," or to Jesus' garden prayer, "[N]ot my will but yours be done," it certainly qualifies as a deep surrender to what God requires of every individual. Joseph did what the Lord commanded him to do, just as Mary and Jesus embraced the Father's will.

All of this is the obedience of faith that St. Paul writes about to the Romans. Paul, identifying himself as a slave and apostle of Jesus, tells of receiving the grace of discipleship. Paul's obedience was experienced as grace and peace. It was the type of obedience that leads to holiness whereby one dedicates one's life to serve others and to God's purposes. In referring to Jesus and the mystery of the resurrection, we realize that Paul put Christ's obedience as a central fact in the paschal mystery. Elsewhere, Paul speaks of Jesus being obedient to the cross, even unto death (Phil 2).

Ahaz had a problem with obedience. When instructed to ask for a sign of the Lord, a sign both deep and high, Ahaz refused under the pretext of tempting the Lord. Isaiah steps in and reprimands Ahaz for wearying the Lord, for a lack of obedience, the obedience of faith. Whether asked or not, God will give a sign. A son will be born of a virgin, a birth that takes place because of the obedience of Mary and Joseph.

John Henry Cardinal Newman once wrote, "Our only safety lies in obedience." Indeed, more than just our safety, for in obedience also lies our peace. Those who listen and do the will of the Father know the peace that exceeds all understanding.

Meditation: What are the similarities and differences between the obedience of Joseph, Mary, and Jesus? What do you see as the relationship between obedience and freedom? Reflect on the moments in your life that were moments of obedience.

Prayer: St. Joseph, intercede for us that we might be obedient as you were in doing what the Lord commands. We are so self-willed; we are so caught up in our own agenda. May we follow your example, and the example of Mary and Jesus, in doing whatever the Father asks of us.

A Good Story

Readings: Isa 7:10-14; Luke 1:26-38

Scripture:
In the sixth month,
   the angel Gabriel was sent from God
   to a town of Galilee called Nazareth,
   to a virgin betrothed to a man named Joseph,
   of the house of David,
   and the virgin's name was Mary. (Luke 1:26-27)

Reflection: In analyzing a story we ask a number of questions: when? where? who? what? why? Our minds are curious in their hunger for knowledge; our hearts are yearning to be stirred. We need a good story as much as we need a good meal.

And here we have it! The time was the sixth month; the place was Nazareth in the country of Galilee; the who question involved many characters: God, an angel, a virgin, an engaged man, an ancient king; and the why dealt with the great mystery of salvation. Stories do not get any better than this.

Our Advent challenge is more than just being familiar with the story and listening to it with renewed attention. Our challenge is to live the story. We must come to realize that God sends messengers into our lives here and now, in this place, at this time. We are to emulate Mary in being open to God's word and in surrendering our lives to God's will. Like Joseph, we need not be afraid, for God's design deserves our trust. And, the why of our life is the same as it was for Mary, Joseph, and David, namely, being instruments of God's love and light.

The Christian story is universal and ubiquitous. It is a story for all seasons and for all cultures. It's all about listening and loving, receiving and sharing, being loved and sharing that grace with others.

But we are not forced to hear or live the story. We have a free will and can turn from light to darkness. King David did that and was called to repentance. We too stand in need of God's mercy. But the grace is always there and the next chapter of the story awaits us. We need but realize that nothing is impossible with God, even our total transformation.

Meditation: How would you summarize the Christian story for small children? What role do you play in God's narrative? What is the "why" of your life?

Prayer: Gracious God, you continue to tell your story of love and forgiveness. We heard it so clearly in the lives of Mary and Joseph; may we now enter into the narrative with all of our mind and heart. Do not let us forget our lines; do not let us forget our mission.

December 21: Tuesday of the Fourth Week of Advent

Attention and Attraction

Readings: Song 2:8-14 or Zeph 3:14-18a; Luke 1:39-45

Scripture:
When Elizabeth heard Mary's greeting,
   the infant leaped in her womb,
   and Elizabeth, filled with the Holy Spirit,
   cried out in a loud voice and said,
   "Most blessed are you among women,
   and blessed is the fruit of your womb." (Luke 1:41-42)

Reflection: A philosophy teacher told his class: "Tell me what you pay attention to, and I will tell you who you are."

Much wisdom here. Even though most of us have a degree of attention deficit disorder, we do pay attention to various things. An analysis of this will indicate our value system. Some people pay attention to money; others, to politics or sports or great music. Some even pay attention to God and when this is done with "loving attention," we are in the presence of a mystic.

Elizabeth paid attention. When Mary greeted Elizabeth something profound happened within her. Joy coursed through her body and soul; even the infant in her womb was moved. You cannot be in the presence of love and not be changed. And the immediate result of love is peace and joy.

Attention, when focused on beauty and goodness, moves us into the land of attraction. Our attention is held spellbound. This happens for some in gazing at a mountain range or the Notre Dame Cathedral in Paris. Apparently, Elizabeth found Mary immensely attractive because of the presence of grace.

Elizabeth caught a glimpse of God's glory and had to cry out in praise. As we near God's immense attractiveness in the nativity of the Lord, we too cannot remain silent. Our attention is caught and God's beauty attracts us. If we surrender to these dispositions, we will be transformed as were Elizabeth and Mary.

Attention deficit disorder and attraction deficit disorder are shortcomings that can diminish our faith. By contrast, when loving attention radiates from our minds and healthy attraction rules our hearts, we are happily vulnerable to God's life of grace.

Meditation: What holds your attention? What do you find attractive? Does your image of God lead to joy or sorrow?

Prayer: Lord Jesus, we ask for the grace of contemplation, that loving attention that so characterized the lives of the mystics. May we be attracted by your glory, power, and beauty. Heal our inattentiveness; purge from us our critical attitudes. Come, Lord Jesus, come.

December 22: Wednesday of the Fourth Week of Advent

Promise of Mercy

Readings: 1 Sam 1:24-28; Luke 1:46-56

Scripture:
"He has come to the help of his servant Israel
    for he remembered his promise of mercy,
    the promise he made to our fathers,
    to Abraham and his children for ever." (Luke 1:54-55)

Reflection: One way of looking at the spiritual life is to invoke the Trinity to come into our lives in a threefold way.

Come, Holy Spirit, come. Grace us with loving attention, joyful mortification, and generous service.

Come, Lord Jesus, come. May we have your wisdom to know what is pleasing to the Father; may we have your heart of affection and love for all; may we have the courage to do the divine will.

Come, Father of the poor, that we may plunge into the mysteries of creation, covenant, and community; that your kingdom might come and your will be done; and all this for your glory.

Grace is a participation in the very life of God. Here is a God who not only creates us but also forms a covenant with us. Part of that covenant is the making and keeping of promises. In sending his Son, God has remembered his promise of love and mercy. It was a promise made to our fathers and mothers of old; it is a promise made by Jesus that the Holy Spirit would be sent, a Spirit of mercy, compassion, and forgiveness. In many ways we experience the fulfillment of that promise in community. People mediate God's mercy to us, and we to them.

Hannah and Mary praised God for the fulfillment of that promise in their lives. Samuel was born of Hannah; Jesus, of Mary. New life and hope filled their lives. Their strong faith led them to proclaim the goodness of God. Their strong love made them resolute in doing God's will.

Advent is a season of hope. It is a time when God's promises are once again realized. Pope Benedict in his letter On Christian Hope reminds us: "The dark door of time, of the future, has been thrown open. The one who hopes lives differently; the one who hopes has been granted the gift of a new life" (*Spe Salvi* 2). Hope is a person; hope is Jesus.

Meditation: What promises have you made? What promises has God made to you? What is your understanding of the notion of covenant?

Prayer: Gracious God, we too sing your praises for your many gifts. These graces are signs of your faithfulness to your promises. You are a God who is with and for us; you are a God of love and mercy. May we participate more fully in your life by making and keeping promises.

Great Expectations—Great Potential

Readings: Mal 3:1-4, 23-24; Luke 1:57-66

Scripture:
All who heard these things took them to heart, saying,
  "What, then, will this child be?
For surely the hand of the Lord was with him." (Luke 1:66)

Reflection: Every child is born with great potential. What that child will ultimately be depends on many circumstances: the home environment, educational opportunities, cultural forces, economic conditions, political climate, and so much more. But ultimately, whether the potential of the child will be realized depends on the "hand of the Lord."

In the case of Elizabeth's child, we know the rest of John the Baptist's story: raised by elderly parents, Zechariah and Elizabeth; called to a prophetic ministry; prepared the way for Jesus; executed after confronting the immoral lifestyle of Herod. John the Baptist grew in age, wisdom, and grace because the Holy Spirit was upon him.

The prophet Malachi reminds us that often the hand of the Lord brings about purification and refinement. So many obstacles block us from reaching our full potential. Sometimes those stumbling blocks are the capital sins: pride, anger, lust, jealousy, sloth, gluttony, or greed. These obstacles involve a turning away from the Lord. Our challenge is to remain open to divine grace and allow the Lord to turn our hearts and minds to truth, goodness, and beauty.

One of the great tragedies of life is to see gifted children (and adults) not reach their full potential. Call it a wasted life or anything else, the world is diminished because of unrealized potential. John the Baptist grew to maturity and did his life's work in just a few years. By doing so, he glorified God. John is a model of discipleship for us.

The principal agent of growth is the Holy Spirit. Thus, the need to invoke that Spirit to enlighten us to see, to enkindle us to be on fire with God's love, and to empower us to live the divine commands. We call this the work of sanctification; we attribute that work to the grace of God's Holy Spirit.

Meditation: What gifts has God given you? Are these gifts being nurtured and shared with others? In what ways has the hand of the Lord been upon you?

Prayer: Gracious God, you are extravagant with your gifts. More, you send your Spirit into our lives to nurture those blessings. Help us to be open to your Spirit and to take responsibility for what you have given us. May we bring you glory by living full, mature lives. Purify our hearts; refine our minds, we pray.

God's Great Oath

Readings: 2 Sam 7:1-5, 8b-12, 14a, 16; Luke 1:67-79

Scripture:
"This was the oath he swore to our father Abraham:
   to set us free from the hand of our enemies,
   free to worship him without fear,
   holy and righteous in his sight
      all the days of our life." (Luke 1:73-75)

Reflection: God's promise of freedom fills us with Advent hope. Though we claim to be a free people, exercising liberty at will, deep down we know that we are not as free as we suppose. Too often we are enslaved by lower instincts such as excessive eating and drinking; too often we are held in bondage psychologically by fears or low self-esteem; and, even spiritually, we can have a distorted concept of God that distances us from divine mercy and love.

God promised Abraham and David that freedom is possible. God himself will set us free so that our worship and prayer will not be based on fear. It is a divine freedom that does two things: makes us holy and makes us righteous. By contrast, living out of fear removes the joy and peace that signify the presence of God's Spirit.

This holiness means that interiorly we live in loving union with our God. This is accomplished through grace, God's self-offer of his Spirit. It is a life of friendship that is both affectionate and demanding. The love God gives us is to be shared. We become, through grace, the recipients and transmitters of divine life. To get caught up in this participation in divine life leads to happiness.

God's freedom also makes us righteous. Because of God's great oath we can now live a moral life that puts us in good relationship with our neighbor. This divine oath also puts us in right relationship with God himself. We are justified by faith; righteousness is essentially a gift—gratuitous, unmerited.

God's oath is incarnated in our feast tomorrow. It is Jesus, through his birth, life, death, and resurrection, who liberates us from sin and calls us to holiness and righteousness. There is no greater gift we can give the Lord than to commit ourselves to participate in his paschal mystery.

Meditation: What do you understand by holiness and righteousness? In what ways have you experienced God's great oath? What addictions do you have to deal with?

Prayer: Lord Jesus, shine on our darkness and guide us on the way to peace. You are the promise of the Father; you are the one who sets us free. May we be always grateful and joyful for your gift of divine life. Make us righteous and holy in your sight.

CHRISTMAS AND DAYS
WITHIN ITS OCTAVE

Vigil Mass: Once upon a Time

Readings: Isa 62:1-5; Acts 13:16-17, 22-25; Matt 1:1-25 or 1:18-25

Scripture:
This is how the birth of Jesus Christ came about.
When his mother Mary was betrothed to Joseph,
  but before they lived together,
  she was found with child through the Holy Spirit.
    (Matt 1:18)

Reflection: There is something about a story that grabs our attention. Who are the people doing this or that? What are the motives for their actions? What happens and why? Will the tale have a happy or sad ending? How does this story reveal something about me?

In a variety of ways, narrative deals with these questions. But there is a unique story—the story of Jesus the Christ— that has changed the world. People of faith truly believe that God became man in the person of Jesus. People of faith believe that this Jesus lived, died, and rose from the dead for our salvation. People of faith believe that if they participate in this great mystery through grace, they, too, will rise with Christ into new and everlasting life.

Is it a true story? Is it too good to be true? Our faith says it is true and it has become the good news of salvation.

At this vigil Mass we listen to how the story unfolds. Matthew gives us the family tree of Jesus and how this child was born into our complex, mysterious human condition. Even his parents, Mary and Joseph, had to struggle with the strangeness of God's plan. We hear in the Acts of the Apostles how St. Paul traveled all over the Mediterranean world telling the story going all the way back to Israel's covenant with the Lord, through the prophets and kings, down to the person of Jesus. Isaiah the prophet adds some more chapters to God's great story of salvation. Isaiah proclaims God's victory and how, on that great day, the people will be vindicated. Even more, the prophet tells us that God rejoices in us.

"Once upon a time . . ." We are to listen up, embrace the story, and live it by being agents of God's love, compassion, and forgiveness. If we do that, then we show that the story is not too good to be true.

Meditation: When did you first comprehend the Christian story? Who told it to you and what impact did it have on your life? To whom have you told the story and what was the reaction of your listeners?

Prayer: Lord Jesus, born of Mary, help us to comprehend the depth of your story. We have heard it so often; we have taken it for granted. Give us fresh eyes to see anew the mystery of your love; give us fresh ears to hear the marvels of your love and mercy for us. And then, give us the grace not only to tell the story but also to live it fully.

Mass at Midnight: Glory to God

Readings: Isa 9:1-6; Titus 2:11-14; Luke 2:1-14

Scripture:
And suddenly there was a multitude of the heavenly host
    with the angel, praising God and saying:
        "Glory to God in the highest
            and on earth peace to those on whom his favor
                rests." (Luke 2:13-14)

Reflection: Glory has something to do with beauty. And what is more beautiful than the overwhelming grace of God coming to dwell with us. Indeed, how could the shepherds not be afraid—"and they were struck with great fear"—when God's glory engulfed them. Here, in the dead of night, the Light had come.

We glorify God by doing what Mary and Joseph did. They embraced God's will and in that surrender they experienced peace despite the fact that they knew all the hardships of a pilgrim's journey: poverty, lack of residence, shortage of life's necessities. By doing what God asked of them, they experienced God's favor and, once having received this participation in the life of grace, they shared it with each other and all whom they met.

Christmas is about glory, God's beauty made manifest in the birth of Jesus. Christmas is about peace, the graced relationship in which we are "right" with God. Christmas is about joy for we have heard the good news of God's love and mercy.

There is nothing romantic in all of this. To the contrary, the Christmas mystery makes immense demands on those who enter salvation history. Essentially, we are to make room in our hearts for the Lord. And when the Lord comes, he comes with work to do—the creative, redemptive, sanctifying work of salvation. We celebrate Christmas not just by attending Eucharist and singing our beautiful Christmas carols; we celebrate Christmas by glorifying God through a loving adoration that puts us at the service of anyone we meet who is in need.

"Glory to God in the highest!" Praise to our God who has given us the Prince of Peace.

Meditation: What does Christmas mean for you? What has been your experience of peace and glory? How can you glorify God this Christmas?

Prayer: Lord Jesus, born of Mary, help us to understand more deeply the mystery of your coming among us. May we glorify you in prayer and service; may we be instruments of your peace and joy. Grant us the grace to do your will, whatever it may be.

Mass at Dawn: Mary's Heart

Readings: Isa 62:11-12; Titus 3:4-7; Luke 2:15-20

Scripture:
And Mary kept all these things,
  reflecting on them in her heart.
Then the shepherds returned,
  glorifying and praising God
  for all they had heard and seen,
  just as it had been told to them. (Luke 2:19-20)

Reflection: Is it possible to understand the Christmas mystery and yet not understand the heart of Mary? Mary took into her affection the great events surrounding the birth of her Son: the journey to Bethlehem, the lack of room in the inn, the manger and the birth itself, the coming of the shepherds, and so much more. In her prayer, she pondered what God had done for her and probably, once again, sang her *Magnificat*, the hymn that Elizabeth heard months before.

And the shepherds? They went back to their people reflecting on this most amazing event. Their reflections broke forth in their own hymn as they glorified and praised God. Once again God made his revelation known to the lowly and the poor. What the shepherds heard and saw would forever change their lives. Their hearts, like Mary's heart, knew the essence of joy: God's love revealed and made manifest.

Not much is said about Joseph and his heart. We know he was a righteous and just man. We can surmise that he was also a person of compassion and affection. His fear was taken away through the message of an angel. His trepidation was conquered by the grace of love. He too must have pondered in his heart all these strange happenings. He too must have glorified and praised God for the birth of Jesus and Mary's well-being.

At the center of the nativity mystery is God's immense love revealed in Jesus. As disciples of the Lord, we are challenged to a contemplative life—a pondering in our hearts of the wonderful things God has done for us. On this feast we do well to glorify and praise God through our personal *Magnificat*.

Meditation: What goes on in your heart? Whom have you shared your faith with? What is your experience of the kindness and generous love of God?

Prayer: Mary, Mother of Jesus and Queen of heaven, pray that we might have a reflective heart. God continues to act in our times. Help us to see the works of his hand and to respond with glory and praise. Our hearts are often narrow and hard. Intercede for us that we may put on the mind and heart of your Son Jesus.

Mass during the Day: Suspicious of Grace

Readings: Isa 52:7-10; Heb 1:1-6; John 1:1-18 or 1:1-5, 9-14

Scripture:
From his fullness we have all received,
   grace in place of grace,
   because while the law was given through Moses,
   grace and truth came through Jesus Christ.
      (John 1:16-17)

Reflection: The insightful author, Madeleine L'Engle, commented that we are often suspicious of grace because we fear "the very lavishness of the gift." I suspect that often when people fall in love they are somewhat leery because the grace of love is so overwhelming.

Another way of saying this is that the good news of Jesus, on this feast of the Nativity, is simply too good to be true. Is it possible that in the beginning the Word Jesus was with God and now has broken into history as the Son of Mary? Is it possible that the vast darkness of human existence is given a light, a Light that will scatter the darkness of sin and even conquer death itself? Is it possible that grace and truth are to be found in the person of Jesus of Nazareth?

But there is more good news. We are the recipients of God's grace, that is, of divine Love, Light, and Life. All of us are offered a share in this richness because God's love is universal and ubiquitous. Now we have seen the very glory of God, light of light, life of life, love of love. In this revelation we are lavished with the very gift of God himself.

We live in a culture of suspicion. Trust is not easily given because too many promises have been made and broken. But our God is faithful. Now in the birth of Christ we are given a new covenant. This love relationship is what John testified to and we are called to do the same. This is the work of evangelization, a significant part of our baptismal call. The grace, the lavish grace, given to us is to be shared with others.

The prophet Isaiah proclaims how beautiful are the feet of those who come bringing glad tidings. In the book of Hebrews, we hear about how God has spoken through his Son and that we are heirs of his life. Grace upon grace; lavish, extravagant, almost too good to be true.

Meditation: Do you have to deal with suspicion in matters of religion? What is your understanding of grace? In what ways do you share God's life with others?

Prayer: Lord Jesus, you are the Word made flesh. Open our hearts to the mystery of your grace. Banish all suspicion from our lives. Give us utter trust and confidence in your word and in your loving mercy. We need your light, your love, and your life.

Qualities of a Holy Family

Readings: Sir 3:2-6, 12-14; Col 3:12-21 or 3:12-17; Matt 2:13-15, 19-23

Scripture:
When the magi had departed, behold,
   the angel of the Lord appeared to Joseph in a dream and
      said,
   "Rise, take the child and his mother, flee to Egypt,
   and stay there until I tell you." (Matt 2:13a)

Reflection: A father, a mother, a child! A family come together for the long haul, be the weather fair or foul. And we have here a "holy" family for it was love that brought and bound them together. It was this graced love that empowered Joseph to assume his heavy responsibility of protecting and providing for Mary and Jesus. It was God's love that enabled Mary to continue her life of obedience and self-giving. It was the Spirit of love that Jesus made manifest in his concern for his parents and the whole world.

   St. Paul reminds us that a family and a community need to be holy. The apostle to the Gentiles writes: "Put on, as God's chosen ones, holy and beloved, heartfelt compassion, kindness, humility, gentleness, and patience, bearing with one another and forgiving one another, if one has a grievance against another; as the Lord has forgiven you, so must you also do" (Col 3:12-13). He then goes on to proclaim that love is the bond of perfection that holds everything together.

Living in close proximity is no easy task. We step on each others' toes; we can so easily be inattentive to others; we are bothered by various eccentricities. Without the presence of the Holy Spirit to assist us, we lose patience, become hard of heart, and even bitter. Family life, meant to be holy and life-giving, turns into an atmosphere of negativity and discord. St. Paul gives us a secret in all of this: be grateful for the blessings given and welcome Christ to dwell deep within us.

Meditation: What do you have to contribute to family life? What qualities do you consider to be essential for a family to be holy? What advice would you give to a newly married couple regarding how they can foster a holy family?

Prayer: Lord Jesus, you lived with Mary and Joseph for so many years. You shared with them your joys and sorrows, your dreams and hopes. Help us to become communities of deep sharing and love. Empower us to be holy and compassionate. Send your Spirit into our hearts and into the heart of our families.

The Call to Be an Evangelist

Readings: 1 John 1-4; John 20:1a, 2-8

Scripture:
On the first day of the week,
    Mary Magdalene ran and went to Simon Peter
    and to the other disciple whom Jesus loved, and told
        them,
    "They have taken the Lord from the tomb,
    and we do not know where they put him."
    (John 20:1a, 2)

Reflection: Mary Magdalene was an evangelist. She ran to tell the disciples of an empty tomb, the news that something strange had happened to the crucified Jesus. Though she did not have information about his whereabouts, she felt impelled to alert the disciples to this mysterious event.

   Later, when the letter of St. John was written, we are given an evangelist's report of what he heard, saw, and touched: the person of Jesus Christ. In this Son of God, eternal life is given to us. In Jesus, eternal life is made visible and available since we have been called into fellowship with him. John had to write of this lest his joy be incomplete.

   One of the deepest longings of the human heart is to share the good things we know. Secrets and knowledge are just waiting to be revealed. We cannot keep good news to ourselves. Evangelists are individuals who have been so touched and moved by grace that they are compelled to go forth, often running, to communicate what they have seen and heard. Are we not all "evangelists" when we have seen a good movie or read a good book and urge others to get to the theater or the bookstore as quickly as possible? And when the message is about a person, the urgency increases tenfold.

Though the feast of Christmas is but two days past, already we are called to be attentive to the Lord's full life in the mystery of the resurrection. It's all about life: birth in Bethlehem and new life after Calvary. It's all about joy, the result of God's love breaking forth as Jesus conquered sin and death. May we see and believe in these mysteries.

Meditation: In what sense are you an evangelist? What good news do you bring to others? Who are the people in your life who brought you the gospel?

Prayer: Lord Jesus, you call us to be disciples and evangelists. Make us more and more aware of your life and love; make us more and more conscious of your abiding presence. In your birth and resurrection, we are given life. In these mysteries, we are given joy.

Power: An Ambivalent Energy

Readings: 1 John 1:5–2:2; Matt 2:13-18

Scripture:
When Herod realized that he had been deceived by the
magi,
he became furious.
He ordered the massacre of all the boys in Bethlehem and
its vicinity
two years old and under. (Matt 2:16a)

Reflection: Power is an ambivalent energy. It can be used
for so much good when those in authority—be they presidents, governors, principals, parents—use it to serve the
well-being of others. Power can be so devastating when it is
self-serving and is used to secure one's own domination and
possessions.

Herod was in power. When news arrived that a child had
been born who would one day become king and ruler, Herod
became furious. In his wrath he destroyed the lives of inno-
cent children. All this in an attempt to protect his domain.
Power misused is deadly both to the victims and, even more,
to the perpetrator who thereby destroys his own humanity.

John's letter speaks about light and darkness, about sin
and forgiveness. Herod walked in darkness and feared the
light. He was unwilling to acknowledge his sin and was not

open to the expiation of sin that Jesus came to bring. Herod lived a lie; he was unconcerned with the truth and justice of things.

By contrast, we witness Joseph, a just and upright man. He lived in the truth and exercised his power as a father to protect life. Though he was not given certitude about the future, he believed and did what God asked of him. We have in Joseph and Herod examples of individuals who made a choice. Joseph chose the light, walking in the ways of the Lord. Herod chose darkness, becoming an agent of death.

The theologian Jon Sobrino maintains that power is God's agent if it leads to love and service. If it is not, power turns into sin.

Meditation: What is your understanding of power? How do you use the energy and power God has given to you? Why is power so ambivalent?

Prayer: Lord Jesus, on this feast of the Holy Innocents, we pray that we might stand in your light. May we one day join the Holy Innocents, who were the objects of Herod's fury. May we never misuse the power you have given us. Send your Spirit of wisdom and courage into our hearts that we may do your will.

December 29: Saint Thomas Becket, Bishop and Martyr
(Catholic Church, optional memorial)

Fifth Day in the Octave of Christmas
(Episcopal Church)

God's Spirit of Light and Love

Readings: 1 John 2:3-11; Luke 2:22-35

Scripture:
Now there was a man in Jerusalem whose name was
   Simeon.
This man was righteous and devout,
   awaiting the consolation of Israel,
   and the Holy Spirit was upon him. (Luke 2:25)

Reflection: There was a man in England whose name was
Thomas Becket (1118–1170). After serving as chancellor to
King Henry II, he became a bishop. When the king attempted
to exercise authority over the church, Thomas Becket resisted
and eventually the king's henchmen murdered Becket in his
own cathedral.

   Through fasting and prayer, Thomas Becket prepared himself for his eventual martyrdom. The Holy Spirit was upon
him, as it was upon Simeon. Both of these men had a vision:
Jesus was a light to the nations. God's Spirit enlightened
Simeon and Becket so that they might understand God's
plan. By contrast, King Henry II lived in darkness. His ambi-

tion for more power and possessions blinded him from comprehending the meaning of life.

During this Christmas season we hear time and time again the theme of light and darkness, of love and hate. Saint Stephen, Saint John the Evangelist, Simeon, and Saint Thomas Becket chose the light. Herod, Henry II, and Saul choose the darkness. Everything depends on the gift of the Holy Spirit. When the Spirit is upon us, we love others and walk in the light; when we refuse to receive God's Spirit, we live in hate and walk in darkness.

The brilliant Dominican theologian Yves Congar once commented that it is the Holy Spirit "that sets things in motion." It was the Holy Spirit that guided Simeon to the temple to encounter the Holy Family; it was the Holy Spirit that strengthened Thomas Becket to confront the king; it is the Holy Spirit, in our lives, who draws us into the light and calls us to be agents of love.

Meditation: What role does the Holy Spirit play in your life? What sets you in motion—for good or ill? Reflect on the people who have been agents of light and love in your life.

Prayer: Come, Holy Spirit, come. Enlighten our minds to see the mystery of Jesus, the light and glory of the nations. Empower us to do the Father's will, whatever the cost. Fill us with the power of love that we might be loving disciples of the Lord Jesus. Come, Holy Spirit, come.

DECEMBER 30–JANUARY 5

Anna's Mission

Readings: 1 John 2:12-17; Luke 2:36-40

Scripture:
She [Anna] never left the temple,
   but worshiped night and day with fasting and prayer.
And coming forward at that very time,
   she gave thanks to God and spoke about the child
   to all who were awaiting the redemption of Jerusalem.
   (Luke 2:37b-38)

Reflection: Before the advent of computer games and other technological wonders, children would often ask their mothers, "What is there for us to do?" Indeed, adults of various ages still ask, in the quietness of their hearts, "What are we to do with the rest of our lives?"

Anna the prophetess, now in her eighties, did not ask that question. She knew what her mission was and fulfilled it. Her callings consisted of three things: fasting, praying, and evangelizing. Anna knew the heart of the spiritual life.

Her first form of worship was mortification. Anna refused the lifestyle of satiation. It was her discipline of mind and body that created an emptiness, which made room for God's grace. Thus, when the Child and his parents arrived at the temple, Anna was prepared and waiting. Fasting opened her to welcome the Babe.

Anna's second form of worship was prayer. Her attention of mind and adherence of heart was centered on the mystery of God. She listened to the stirrings of the Spirit; she responded to the call of God. Both her fasting and prayer were constant—day and night. Both her discipline and adoration were responses to God's gracious intervention.

Anna's mission involved a third component: telling! Her message was about salvation and deliverance. Anna told of this Child who would set Israel free. Hers was the work of evangelization and we are the recipients of the good news.

What are we to do? Anna is a good mentor; Anna is a good model.

Meditation: What role do fasting, prayer, and evangelization play in your life? To whom have you told the good news of Jesus? How does your mission in life compare to that of Anna's?

Prayer: Lord Jesus, you call us to a life of discipline, prayer, and evangelization. Send your Spirit into our minds and hearts so that we might respond to our baptismal call. May we, night and day, turn to you for help; may we, night and day, tell others of your love and mercy.

Life, Light, Love

Readings: 1 John 2:18-21; John 1:1-18

Scripture:
What came to be through him was life,
   and this life was the light of the human race;
   the light shines in the darkness,
   and the darkness has not overcome it. (John 1:4-5)

Reflection: Flannery O'Connor (1925–1964), one of the finest Catholic writers of the twentieth century, authored stories of people who were often grotesque and filled with dark motives. Yet, a constant image throughout her many short stories was the sun, constantly bringing light (and life) even into the darkest of human experiences. In a letter to a friend, O'Connor said that upon reflection all her stories were about the action of grace.

And what is grace if not light and life and, yes, love. God's Word came into history to bring us life, life that will never end. Jesus came to bring light, and all the prophets, including John, testified to the light of God. And when the Word became flesh, we now had a visible manifestation of God's glory, the expression of love.

The Christmas mystery, with its birth of a babe (life) and a star filling the night (light) and gifts being given (love), is an invitation to all of us to both testify to God's presence in our lives as well as commit ourselves to being agents of divine grace. This was the mission of John. Many believed through his testimony; many were enlightened by his preaching and his call to repentance.

The gospel cries out: "From his fullness we have all received, grace in place of grace, because while the law was given through Moses, grace and truth came through Jesus Christ" (John 1:16-17). Here is the source and expression of God's glory; here is the central fact of all history. Our reception of God's fullness demands emptiness. By creating space and having a heart of hospitality, the Lord will come and dwell with us and within us.

Meditation: In what ways can you give testimony to God's grace? What is your understanding of the glory of God? How do you deal with the darkness of history?

Prayer: Lord Jesus, you are the glory of the Father. Open our minds and hearts to the mystery of your life and love. Only then will we be fit instruments of your light. May we give testimony to your grace on our pilgrim journey.

Mary: The Blessed One

Readings: Num 6:22-27; Gal 4:4-7; Luke 2:16-21

Scripture:
"The LORD bless you and keep you!
The LORD let his face shine upon
   you, and be gracious to you!
The LORD look upon you kindly and
   give you peace!" (Num 6:24-26)

Reflection: Is there any greater bliss than to be looked upon with love? Here is a supreme blessing that overflows into joy and peace. When the loving gaze is not experienced, but rather a frown or contempt, what anxiety fills our days. It is difficult to overstate the significance of being seen lovingly.

Mary, the Mother of Jesus, knew herself to be loved. God's gaze fell upon her and new life flowed through her being. She was indeed the highly favored one, called to be a unique instrument in God's plan of salvation. The blessing that she received she passed on to others by her loving gaze and gracious love.

Mary pondered many things in her heart: the message of the angel Gabriel, her visitation to Elizabeth, the birth of her

Son, and his ministry, death, and resurrection. Her heart was full of memories, some of great joy and others of searing pain. In those reflections, like the shepherds who came to honor Mary's newborn son, the Mother of Jesus praised and glorified God. Contemplation led to worship, and worship in turn overflowed into service.

St. Paul resembled Mary in this reflective way of life. In his many letters, he shared with the various faith communities the action of God's grace. To the Galatians he wrote, "God sent the Spirit of his Son into our hearts, crying out, 'Abba, Father!'" (Gal 4:6b). It was this Spirit that dwelt in the heart of Mary, in the heart of St. Paul, indeed, in the heart of the praising and glorifying shepherds.

May the Lord look upon all of us with kindness and give us peace as we enter the New Year with Mary as our model and guide.

Meditation: What has been the greatest blessing in your life? Did it have something to do with being loved? How do you bless others?

Prayer: Lord Jesus, we honor your Mother who reflected so deeply on the favors your Father bestowed on her. Like Mary, may we ponder your kindness; like Mary, may we live lives of obedience and self-giving. Grant us the grace to experience your indwelling Spirit.

The Stewardship of God's Grace

Readings: Isa 60:1-6; Eph 3:2-3a, 5-6; Matt 2:1-12

Scripture:
You have heard of the stewardship of God's grace
   that was given to me for your benefit,
    namely, that the mystery was made known to me by
    revelation. (Eph 3:2)

Reflection: Everyone is given the privilege and duty of being a steward of God's grace. Doctors and principals, parents and professors, farmers and writers, bus drivers and tour guides—everyone is called upon to use their unique gifts in enriching the lives of others. This stewardship, this receiving, nurturing, and sharing of God's love and life, is a way of life and involves serious accountability.

    Isaiah was a steward of God's grace. His sanctified vision called people to realize what is possible if we live in accord with God's design. The prophet speaks of how the Lord's light scatters the darkness of the earth, how all people will come into the Lord's presence, how hearts will throb and overflow with joy. One need but read a novel like Cormac McCarthy's *Blood Meridian* to witness an unsanctified vision in which murder, rape, and scalping are a way of life. Isaiah offers an alternative to history's violence and war.

St. Paul was a steward of God's grace. His unique contribution was the result of a revelation in which God's mystery promised salvation to all. Paul's vision of our unity in Christ expressed the universality of God's love and mercy. God's plan, revealed even more fully by Jesus, is that no one be lost.

The magi too were stewards of God's grace. The story is familiar. As stewards, the magi brought their gifts—gold, frankincense, and myrrh—and offered them to the child born of Mary. Here is stewardship in action: the receiving and sharing of gifts. Of course, the ultimate gift is the gift of self. In Jesus, we are given God's supreme gift—God's self-giving love. This gift is for all. Once again we are given the vision of revelation.

Meditation: In what way are you called to be a steward of God's grace. What is your unique gift? Do you have a sanctified vision of God's plan of salvation?

Prayer: St. Paul, pray for us. Help us to see the revelation of God's love and mercy in Jesus. Intercede for us that we might be fit instruments of God's grace. Too often our vision is dark and without hope. Pray that we might see with the eyes of Christ.

Faith and Love

Readings: 1 John 3:22–4:6; Matt 4:12-17, 23-25

Scripture:
He went around all of Galilee,
    teaching in their synagogues, proclaiming the Gospel of
        the Kingdom,
    and curing every disease and illness among the people.
        (Matt 4:23)

Reflection: There are basically two things that are asked of the disciple of Jesus: belief in him and love for one another. Faith and Love! Here are the cornerstones of our spirituality. When we live out these virtues, we participate in the epiphanies of God.

To believe in the name and person of Jesus means that we be attentive to his teachings. There is no better summary of Jesus' instructions than the Beatitudes (Matt 5:1-12) and the last judgment scene (Matt 25). These bookends of Matthew's gospel offer a vision of happiness and a lifestyle that expresses authentic discipleship. Jesus' words are as fresh today as they were thousands of years ago.

To believe is to embrace and live the proclamation of the gospel. This is the work of evangelization. By witnessing to gospel values we demonstrate our faith. Essentially, that way of life is to hear about God's love and mercy in Christ and then to share those gifts with all whom we meet. Proclamation happens in actions as much as it does in words. In fact, living in accord with gospel words means that our discipleship is truly authentic.

Jesus cured. Jesus healed. Jesus saved. It is in his name that we experience God's redemption. Be our illness physical, psychological, or spiritual, Jesus is deeply concerned that we be made whole. He came among us to bring life, life that will last. All of us stand in need of healing; all of us stand in need of having compassion for our hurting sisters and brothers.

Faith is expressed in love. By having active concern for others, we emulate the life and ministry of Jesus. By loving, we honor the name of Jesus and give glory to his Father.

Meditation: How deep is your faith, your love? What is the relationship between these two theological virtues? How do you honor the name of Jesus?

Prayer: Lord Jesus, blessed be your name. Open our ears to your teaching; open our hearts to your Gospel; open our hands to express your compassion. Grant us, in your mercy, the grace of love. We need ask for nothing more.

January 4: Saint Elizabeth Ann Seton
(Catholic Church)

Knowing God

Readings: 1 John 4:7-10; Mark 6:34-44

Scripture:
Beloved, let us love one another,
    because love is of God;
    everyone who loves is begotten by God and knows God.
Whoever is without love does not know God, for God is
    love. (1 John 4:7-8)

Reflection: St. Elizabeth Ann Seton (1774–1821) was canonized in 1975. She understood and lived the words of St. John. In her heart and life she knew that love comes from God; indeed, God is love. Her educational work among the poor and immigrants in the United States was an expression of that love.

In the end, it's all about feeding. Providing food for the body, the mind, and the soul was the mission of Jesus. When Jesus saw the crowds his heart was stirred with compassion for he knew their lostness, their hunger, and their deepest desires. The miracle of the multiplication of the five loaves and two fish is yet another sign of Jesus' love for people. That feeding continues day in and day out as we gather at the eucharistic table.

One of the most significant questions in the spiritual life is: "How do we come to know the mystery of God?" There is an intellectual component to this question. Through revelation, study, and prayer, we can grow in our knowledge of the Trinity. Scripture and tradition are two key paths in coming to know our God.

Yet there is another way, the way of the heart. Since God is love, we come to know God by being loving people. Philosophers call this type of knowing knowledge by connaturality. The person who has no formal education and is even illiterate can come to know God by living God's life, that is, by receiving God's love and giving it away. Such a person probably has no language system to describe who God is, but that person knows by way of imitation.

One need but think of St. Thérèse of Lisieux (1873–1897) who died at the age of twenty-four. Her knowledge of God, though influenced by Scripture and the writings of some spiritual masters, was primarily by way of experience. It was love given her and lived that drew her into mysticism, an immediate, unmediated experience of the Trinity.

Meditation: How much formal study have you had regarding the nature of God? How has God been revealed to you through loving people? What do you understand when you hear that God is love?

Prayer: Loving God, fill our hearts with the grace of your love. May we come to know you and live your life. Forgive our selfishness; remove our blindness; stir our hearts with compassion. Knowledge of you is life itself. Send your Spirit into our lives.

January 5: Saint John Neumann, Bishop
(Catholic Church)

Fears: Graced and Otherwise

Readings: 1 John 4:11-18; Mark 6:45-52

Scripture:
There is no fear in love,
  but perfect love drives out fear
  because fear has to do with punishment,
  and so one who fears is not yet perfect in love.
    (1 John 4:18)

Reflection: In his biography on St. Augustine, Peter Brown states, "Yet, like so many men, Augustine feared the sea." There is a wise fear here. The sea can be treacherous and deadly. Only those who lack experience of the sea or are simply ignorant of its dangers lack respect for large bodies of water.

The disciples are out at sea and confront a double fear: fear of the stormy sea itself and fear of an apparent ghost. Then, they hear those glorious words that ring down through the ages in the hearts of all believers: "Take courage, it is I, do not be afraid!" (Mark 6:50b). These phrases were embedded in the heart of Pope John Paul II as he traveled the world far and wide and instructed youths that they ought not be afraid.

There is a graced, reverential fear, one that is concerned with offending God in any way. But there are other fears that flow from a lack of trust in God's providential care. What is needed is love, a self-giving that relies on grace and God's abiding presence.

One need but think of a mother who runs into the burning home to rescue her children. Her love drives out all fear and enables her to risk her life in the face of almost certain death. It is this type of love, one that knows no limits, that God gives to us. Jesus rushes into history, into certain death, in order to save us from sin and death. Divine courage does not hesitate before all the evil in the world. As disciples of this Lord, we are invited to follow in his way and live courageous lives. It is in the paschal mystery, this living and dying with Jesus, that we find our joy and peace.

Meditation: What are the fears in your life? What is the relationship between love and courage? Why is the practice of the presence of God so important in dealing with the trials and temptations of life?

Prayer: Lord Jesus, you tell us not to fear. Yet, there are so many dangers on this human journey. Too often we forget your presence and feel abandoned and vulnerable. Deepen your gift of faith in our hearts; deepen your gift of trust that fear might be banished once for all.

EPIPHANY AND
BAPTISM OF THE LORD

January 6: Epiphany
(Episcopal Church, see January 2)

Jesus: God's Divine Poem

Readings: 1 John 4:19–5:4; Luke 4:14-22a

Scripture:
Jesus returned to Galilee in the power of the Spirit,
   and news of him spread throughout the whole region.
He taught in their synagogues and was praised by all.
   (Luke 4:14-15)

Reflection: In 2001, Harmony Books published *Ten Poems to Change Your Life* written by Roger Housden. Using the works of such poets as Mary Oliver, Antonio Machado, Walt Whitman, Rumi, Pablo Neruda, St. John of the Cross, and others, Housden presents their poetry and then gives his own commentary regarding his understanding of the verse.

Poetry has power, the power to change our life. Jesus is the Poem of the Father, a divine verse that incarnates the mystery of divine love and mercy. Our task is to study the meaning of his ministry and life.

We read in Scripture how Jesus was anointed by the Spirit and it was the Spirit's power that governed his work. His mission was one of proclaiming liberty, bringing good news, healing the blind, freeing the oppressed. To understand this poetry and to emulate this ministry is to change.

Whence comes transformation? In the first letter of St. John we are told God first loved us. Here is the power of the

Spirit that anointed Jesus and who anoints us in baptism and confirmation. It is a power that enables us to love our sisters and brothers; it is a power that enables us to hear and abide by God's commandments. This transformation is truly amazing.

Nor need we wait for this transformation to happen at some later date. "Today this Scripture passage is fulfilled in your hearing" (Luke 4:21b). In word and sacrament, Jesus is with us now. He is *the* poem capable of changing our personal life and the very life of the world. In coming to bring us the fullness of life, Jesus has blazed the trail.

Meditation: What are some of the major changes in your life? Has poetry ever been one of the causes? Has Jesus' life, death, and resurrection led you to a personal transformation?

Prayer: Lord Jesus, give us a portion of your Spirit. Anoint us with the oil of gladness that we may be transformed into your disciples. May we put on your mind and heart; may we love our sisters and brothers as you have loved us. Come, Lord Jesus, come.

January 7

Wish List

Readings: 1 John 5:5-13; Luke 5:12-16

Scripture:
It happened that there was a man full of leprosy in one of
    the towns where Jesus was;
    and when he saw Jesus,
    he fell prostrate, pleaded with him, and said,
    "Lord, if you wish, you can make me clean." (Luke 5:12)

Reflection: Wish lists come with a variety of items. There are
physical wishes such as the longing for good health and a
long life; there are psychological wishes in that we yearn for
friendships and recognition; and, there are spiritual wishes
that would include deep union with God and a sense of
peace. Our wish lists are long and diverse.

The fulfillment of our desires is thwarted by illness (leprosy), by rejection, by sin. All of us need cleansing and purification. If we but ask, we can be assured that Jesus is
saying to us today: "I do will it. Be made clean" (Luke 5:13b).
God's will is that we have fullness of life, indeed, life in
abundance (John 10:10).

In order for this cleansing to happen, there are several
dispositions needed: humility, courage, and hope. Humility
means that we face the truth of our human condition. If we
are truly honest, we must admit to the leprosy of our minds

and hearts. This illness takes the form of prejudices and big-otry, hardness of heart and insensitivity. We stand in need of forgiveness and healing. No one is exempt.

This cleansing also demands courage, the courage to change. Transformation is painful as we are stripped of what was for what might be. The unknown causes fear. The grace needed here is trust in the Lord. Our God is a God of life and love. We have nothing to fear.

Hope is a third element on our pilgrim journey. The lexi-con of hope includes a deep sense of the possible, realistic expectations, and enthusiasm. When the heart is hopeful, great things can happen.

Meditation: What purifications are needed in your life? Why are humility and courage foundational to the spiritual jour-ney? What are your deepest longings, your most significant wishes?

Prayer: Lord Jesus, you will that we be clean and whole. Touch our lives with your healing forgiveness. Strengthen us to face our leprosy, whatever form it takes. You are the Lord of life and love. Come quickly to our aid.

The Best Man's Duty

Readings: 1 John 5:14-21; John 3:22-30

Scripture:
"The one who has the bride is the bridegroom;
   the best man, who stands and listens for him,
   rejoices greatly at the bridegroom's voice.
So this joy of mine has been made complete.
He must increase; I must decrease." (John 3:29-30)

Reflection: "Stay out of the way" is the motto for best men, vice presidents, and those who play second fiddle. It's all about knowing one's place. John the Baptist was keenly aware that his mission was one of preparation. He pointed to the Christ and got out of the way.

The wedding analogy is most appropriate. When the bridal party comes into the banquet hall and the couples are introduced, everyone is waiting for the bride and groom themselves. The spotlight shifts from the attendants to the newlyweds. Just so, as Jesus comes baptizing in the Holy Spirit, it is time for John to make his exit. As so often happens in Christian history, the exit is one of martyrdom. In life John served God's purpose as he did in his death.

All ordained ministers and all lay ministers should have as their motto: "He must increase; I must decrease." In other words, "It's not about us!" Ministry is about the kingdom and giving glory to God. Yet we all know from personal experience that the ego keeps getting in the way. How am I doing? How am I coming across?

The major consequence of doing our duty with love and knowing our proper place is joy. It is that inner affective mood that says this is good, this is very good. Be it visiting a nursing home, proclaiming the gospel, giving that cup of cold water, fasting, or praying, we have a sense of fittingness. We are doing God's will. In that is our joy and peace. To do this ourselves is partial joy; when the community does it together, our joy will be complete.

Meditation: What is your place in God's plan? How have you shared your joy of faith with others? Do you find it hard to stay out of the way?

Prayer: Lord Jesus, may you become the center of our lives. Too often we get caught up in ourselves, in a narrow narcissism. Give us the grace to decrease in our sense of self-importance. Help us to increase our faith in you. Only then will our joy be complete and our peace whole.

January 9: The Baptism of the Lord

A Permanent Invitation

Readings: Isa 42:1-4, 6-7; Acts 10:34-38; Matt 3:13-17

Scripture:
Jesus came from Galilee to John at the Jordan
   to be baptized by him.
John tried to prevent him, saying,
   "I need to be baptized by you,
   and yet you are coming to me?" (Matt 3:13-14)

Reflection: According to Jesuit Fr. Francois Roustang, there are not many Christians who consider baptism to be "a permanent invitation" to live in close intimacy with the Lord who waits for them. Whether the numbers are few or many, baptism is the sacrament of initiation into the life of Christ, the Christ who waits for a response in faith.

John the Baptist invited people to repentance. By turning away from the darkness of sin and into the light of God's presence, joy and peace awaited them. Jesus invited people into the realm of God's kingdom, a kingdom of truth and life, of holiness and grace, of justice, love, and peace.

Why is it that the invitation, so constant and permanent, is not eagerly accepted? Why is it that close intimacy with the mystery of God is shunned? Perhaps the answer lies in the fact that within the invitation to be baptized are a number of demanding imperatives. And when an invitation involves imperatives one can hear the feet making for the exit.

104   *Epiphany and Baptism of the Lord*

What imperatives? Be mature! Be holy! Serve! Embrace community! Be generous! These are all components in the life of discipleship. To follow in the way of Jesus, this life of grace, one is called to grow up, to be loving, to care for others, to reject individualism, to sacrificially give one's time, talent, and treasure. Granted, the grace necessary to live this baptismal life is given in the sacrament and supplemented by the sacraments of confirmation and Eucharist, but it is a life of self-giving that underlies this "permanent invitation."

Jesus came to bring us the fullness of life, to reconcile all of creation to the Father, to renew the face of the earth. We are baptized into this life. We are invited into the eternal joy and peace of God's abiding love.

Meditation: What is your understanding of baptism? Is it "a permanent invitation?" Which of the imperatives of baptism do you find difficult?

Prayer: Lord Jesus, the beloved of the Father, we are grateful for the invitation to participate in the mystery of your life and love. May we say yes to your call and rejoice in the intimacy of your Father's will. May our sharing in your life of self-giving bring about your kingdom here on earth.